UNOFFICIAL

TAYLOR IN LONDON

UNOFFICIAL

TAYLOR IN LONDON

THE FAN'S GUIDE TO THE CITY

CONTENTS

SOUTH LONDON

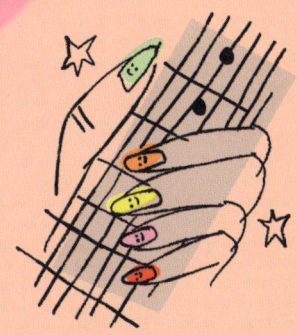

WEST LONDON

BEYOND LONDON 116

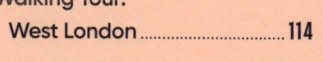

INTRODUCTION

There's always been an invisible string pulling Taylor back to London. It's a city she's called home, a place that's inspired song lyrics and the backdrop for one or two dates (ahem). She's made lasting memories with fans here too, with iconic performances at Wembley Stadium, the O2 and even Eventim Apollo back in the day. They've been cheering her on since her first visit across the pond, and chances are, if you're reading this, you're one of them.

Taylor in London will have you following in Taylor's footsteps: you'll find the restaurants she's eaten in, the places she's hinted at in songs and the sights she's shown up in. Some are well known, others might surprise you. And, well, we've included some fan favourites, even if the link is a little harder to prove (did she really spend time there? Who knows, we're going with it).

So grab your polaroid camera and your red scarf, pop on some friendship bracelets and explore the city, Taylor-style.

Are you ready for it?

LONDON

LONDON ON THE MAP

A

B

HIGHGATE
p 66

THE FLASK
p 68

HAMPSTEAD HEATH
p 60

THE HOLLY BUSH
p 58

THE GARDEN GATE
p 56

1

WEMBLEY STADIUM
p 112

WILLESDEN

HARLESDEN

ST JOHN'S WOOD

PRIMROSE HILL
p 44

ABBEY ROAD STUDIOS
p 40

LONDON ZOO
p 42

LORD'S CRICKET GROUND
p 38

CASA CRUZ
p 108

ALICE'S
p 106

WHITE CITY

NOTTING HILL

HYDE PARK
p 100

ACTON

SHEPHERD'S BUSH

KENSINGTON PALACE
p 104

HAMMERSMITH

EVENTIM APOLLO
p 110

VICTORIA AND ALBERT MUSEUM
p 98

CHELSEA

2

CHISWICK

BENIHANA CHELSEA
p 96

FULHAM

BATTERSEA

PUTNEY

A

B

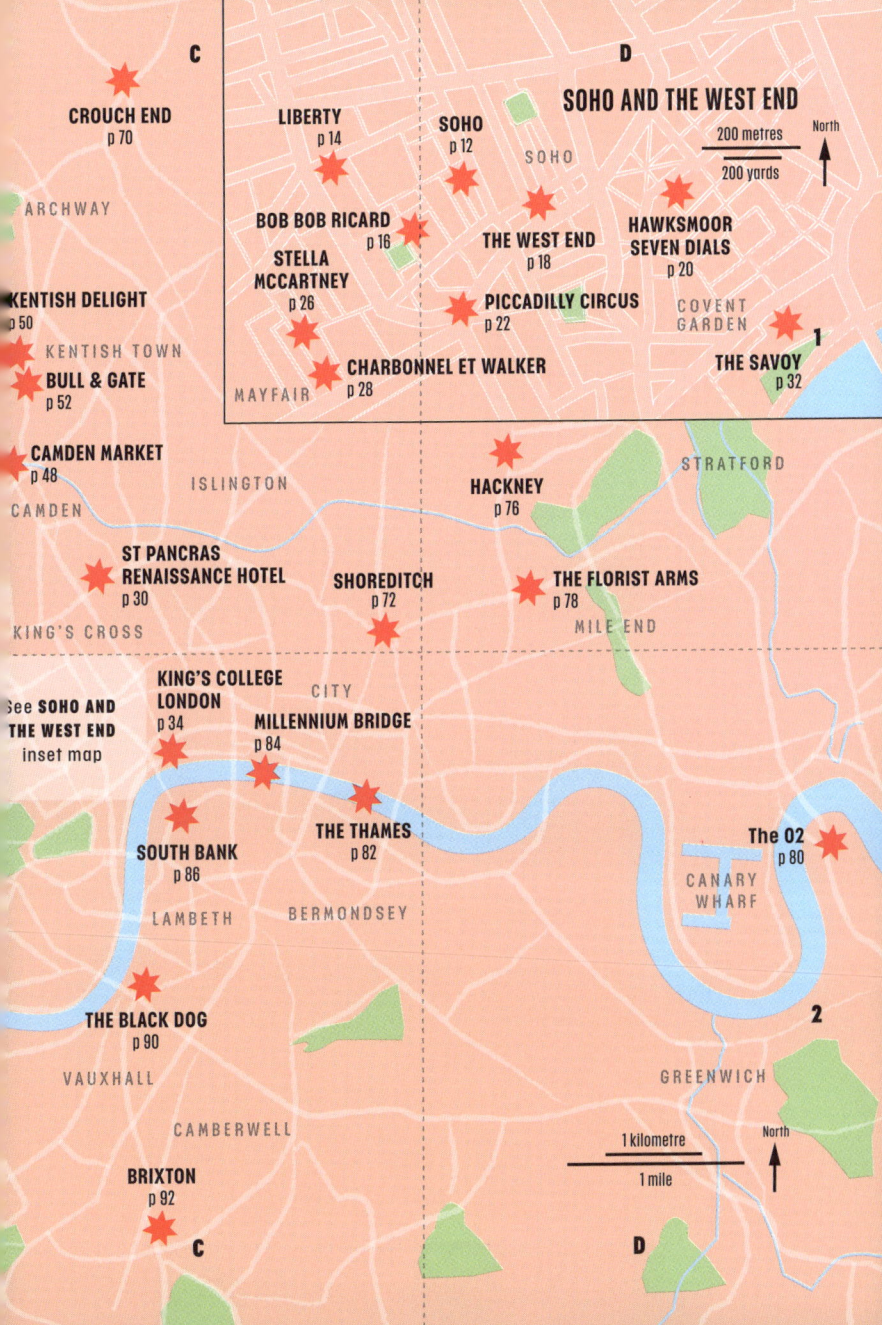

SOHO AND THE WEST END

200 metres

200 yards

North

C

CROUCH END
p 70

ARCHWAY

LIBERTY
p 14

SOHO
p 12

SOHO

D

BOB BOB RICARD
p 16

STELLA McCARTNEY
p 26

THE WEST END
p 18

HAWKSMOOR SEVEN DIALS
p 20

KENTISH DELIGHT
p 50

BULL & GATE
p 52

KENTISH TOWN

PICCADILLY CIRCUS
p 22

COVENT GARDEN

1

CHARBONNEL ET WALKER
p 28

THE SAVOY
p 32

CAMDEN MARKET
p 48

MAYFAIR

CAMDEN

ISLINGTON

HACKNEY
p 76

STRATFORD

ST PANCRAS RENAISSANCE HOTEL
p 30

SHOREDITCH
p 72

THE FLORIST ARMS
p 78

KING'S CROSS

MILE END

See **SOHO AND THE WEST END** inset map

KING'S COLLEGE LONDON
p 34

CITY

MILLENNIUM BRIDGE
p 84

THE THAMES
p 82

The O2
p 80

SOUTH BANK
p 86

LAMBETH

BERMONDSEY

CANARY WHARF

THE BLACK DOG
p 90

VAUXHALL

2

CAMBERWELL

GREENWICH

1 kilometre

1 mile

North

BRIXTON
p 92

C

D

SOHO

A lively London neighbourhood, Soho is a treasure trove of independent restaurants, vintage boutiques and welcoming LGBTQ+ bars. The area is worth visiting any time of the day but its personality shines at night, when neon signs glow against elegant Georgian architecture and crowds descend on the streets in search of a good dance floor. Soho's effortlessly cool vibe also attracts big names, though celebrities often seek shelter in exclusive private members' clubs, such as Soho House and The Groucho Club. It was the latter that Taylor was seen visiting in 2013 with British singer-songwriter Tom Odell. If shopping's more your thing, swing by nearby Carnaby Street. This colourful pedestrianized street is associated with Britain's swinging sixties and rebellious fashion. With so much to see and experience in Soho, it's no wonder this special quarter got name-dropped on Taylor's *Lover* album.

📍 D1 · 🏠 W1 · 🚇 Oxford Circus, Piccadilly Circus

LIBERTY

Liberty has been a go-to spot for luxury shopping since 1875, and is best known for its gorgeous paisley "Liberty Print" fabrics. Not that it's all about textiles, mind. These days you'll find everything from high-end fashion to stylish homeware spread across six spacious floors. And did we mention the grade II-listed building? It's stunning, making the store a must-visit even if you don't plan on splashing the cash. As for the Taylor connection: in 2015, the singer revealed in an interview with *ELLE* that a trip here inspired her to write the song "Clean", which later featured on the *1989* album. The flagship store, with its impressive wooden beams, nooks and crannies proved to be the magical distraction for a broken heart and a place to find closure. Taylor recalled stepping out onto the London streets after browsing inside and having a moment of realization: she hadn't thought about her former flame once. So whether you're looking to ease heartache or simply buy a new wardrobe staple, Liberty is *the* place for (retail) therapy.

📍 C1 · 🏠 Regent Street, W1B 5AH
🕐 10am–8pm Mon–Sat & public hols, midday–6pm Sun
Ⓦ libertylondon.com

BOB BOB RICARD

One thing's for sure: you won't experience any champagne problems at Bob Bob Ricard. This iconic venue claims to pour more champagne than any other restaurant in Britain. Located a stone's throw from busy Piccadilly Circus (*p22*), it's the perfect venue to celebrate with friends or enjoy an indulgent pre-theatre meal. Order caviar and lobster from the comfort of the plush leather booths, which are inspired by the sumptuous interiors of the Orient Express, then simply hold down the gold "Press for Champagne" button – each table is fitted with one to ensure glasses are never empty. Taylor visited this glamourous spot for actor Joe Alwyn's birthday in 2020, along with award-winning singer Ed Sheeran, Taylor's long-established friend. It's unclear what brand of fizz took their fancy that evening but today the drinks menu includes at least 30 varieties of champagne, from Moët & Chandon to Dom Pérignon.

📍 C1 • 🏠 1 Upper James Street, W1F 9DF
🚇 Piccadilly Circus • 🕐 5pm–midnight Mon–Tue, midday–3pm & 5pm–midnight Wed–Thu, midday–midnight Fri–Sun • Ⓦ bobbobricard.com/soho

THE WEST END

London has always enjoyed a wonderful theatrical tradition, particularly in the West End. The city's answer to Broadway is home to around 40 theatres, showing acclaimed musicals, record-breaking plays and new productions. Celebrities are no strangers to treading the boards, drawing in crowds that had previously only had the opportunity to see them on screen. Sometimes they even attract members of their friendship group. In summer 2024, Taylor went to see friend Cara Delevingne perform as Sally Bowles in the West End show *Cabaret*. The two caught up backstage, sharing a picture online. While Taylor has yet to perform in a West End production herself, she has been labelled by fans as a "theatre kid" after old videos of her performing as Maria in *The Sound of Music* emerged online. Taylor also indulged in her passion for cats by appearing in the film adaptation of Andrew Lloyd Webber's musical *Cats*. This feline-themed stage production debuted in the West End in 1981, closing 21 years later.

———————

📍 D1 • 🏠 W1 • 🚇 Leicester Square, Charing Cross
Ⓦ officiallondontheatre.com

HAWKSMOOR SEVEN DIALS

An upscale steakhouse, Hawksmoor Seven Dials has become an institution thanks to its quality cuts, sustainable seafood and indulgent side dishes. Insatiable Brits can't get enough of its menu and Hawksmoor now has an empire spreading across London and the UK. Taylor and Joe Alwyn were seen leaving the Covent Garden branch after a romantic dinner date in 2018. The singer wore a green off-the-shoulder dress, drawing attention to her necklace. Engraved with the letter J, presumably for Joe, the chain is widely speculated to be the one referenced in the song "Call It What You Want". Taylor later revisited letter-themed accessories for the 2025 Grammy Awards, when she wore a red "T" letter charm on her leg. This stylistic choice was a little less clear cut, as fans debated whether the "T" stood for Taylor or boyfriend Travis Kelce. Now there's something to chew over.

———————

📍 D1 • 🏠 11 Langley Street, WC2H 9JG
🚆 Charing Cross • Ⓜ Covent Garden
🕐 11:45am–10:30pm Mon–Thu, 11:45am–11pm Fri–Sat, 11:45am–10pm Sun
Ⓦ thehawksmoor.com/locations/seven-dials

PICCADILLY CIRCUS

It may be a tourist hotspot but Piccadilly Circus is always worth a visit, especially after dark, when its digital advertisements are at their most dazzling. The area is rarely quiet – street performers entertain crowds, and red London buses and black cabs chug through busy roads. Demanding even more attention? Fireworks, of course, or at least that's what happened in Taylor's city-hopping "End Game" music video. As the singer danced on the top floor of a double-decker London bus, fireworks illuminated the area's grand buildings. Come and see them for yourself (pyrotechnics not included), then venture off to explore more of central London – Leicester Square and Trafalgar Square are but a walk away.

📍 D1 · 🏠 W1 · 🚇 Leicester Square, Charing Cross
ⓦ visitlondon.com

STELLA MCCARTNEY

Taylor has long been a fan of Stella McCartney's sustainable and timeless creations. In 2019, the duo joined forces to create a range of limited edition merchandise to complement the release of *Lover*. Items included T-shirts featuring Taylor's pet cat, rainbow tie-dye sweatshirts and pastel-coloured accessories. Her appreciation for Paul McCartney's daughter also led to a special shoutout in the song "London Boy", followed by another collaboration in 2020 for *Evermore* and *Folklore*: both album covers see Taylor wearing stylish Stella McCartney coats. Taylor's love affair with the brand seeps into her personal life, too – she is regularly snapped wearing skirts, coats and blazers by the eco-conscious designer. Today, the singer is more likely to swing by Stella McCartney's corporate office in West London but the flagship store on Bond Street is perfect for fans looking to emulate Taylor's style. Just be prepared to leave with a dent in your bank account – these chic outfits aren't for the budget-conscious.

📍 C1 • 🏠 23 Old Bond Street, W1S 4PZ
🚇 Piccadilly Circus, Green Park • 🕐 10:30am–6:30pm
Mon–Sat, midday–6pm Sun • ⓦ stellamccartney.com

CHARBONNEL ET WALKER

Sweet-toothed fans are in for a treat with a visit to this historic chocolate shop. Established in 1875, Charbonnel et Walker is regarded as Britain's first luxury chocolatier. Today, there are several stores across London but the Bond Street branch is one of the best. Nestled in a gorgeous Victorian arcade among a range of exclusive independent shops, Charbonnel et Walker is easy to spot thanks to its beautiful window displays. Inside, visitors can browse rows of attractive gift boxes and peer at small pyramids of handmade truffles behind glass counters. This is, of course, exactly what Taylor did in 2012. She braved the British weather to visit the prestigious Bond Street store, leaving with several ribboned boxes of melt-in-the-mouth chocolates. Why not follow in her footsteps?

📍 C1 • 🏠 One, 28 The Royal Arcade, Old Bond Street, W1S 4BT
🚇 Piccadilly Circus, Green Park • 🕐 10am–6:30pm Mon–Sat,
11:30am–5:30pm Sun • Ⓦ charbonnel.co.uk

ST PANCRAS RENAISSANCE HOTEL

For some, the St Pancras Renaissance Hotel is an incredible 150-year-old Gothic masterpiece; for others it's where Taylor's "I Don't Wanna Live Forever (Fifty Shades Darker)" music video was filmed. Teaming up with singer and former One Directioner Zayn Malik, Taylor captures the essence of a tortured and frustrated lover, pacing along dark, atmospheric hotel corridors and smashing a hotel mirror. It's a noirish departure from the pop band Spice Girls' approach, who filmed the upbeat "Wannabe" music video at this iconic red-brick hotel in 1996. While you're in the area, make sure to take a look around. The hotel is a short distance from Coal Drops Yard, a popular shopping and dining district, as well as the pretty Regent's Canal. And, if listening to Taylor's "Paris" has you thinking about a trip to the city of love, you don't have to go far. St Pancras Renaissance Hotel is conveniently located in St Pancras International train station, with regular Eurostar services running to France's capital.

📍 C1 · 🏠 St Pancras International, Euston Road, N1C 4QP
🚇 Kings Cross St Pancras · 🕐 Daily · ⓦ marriot.com

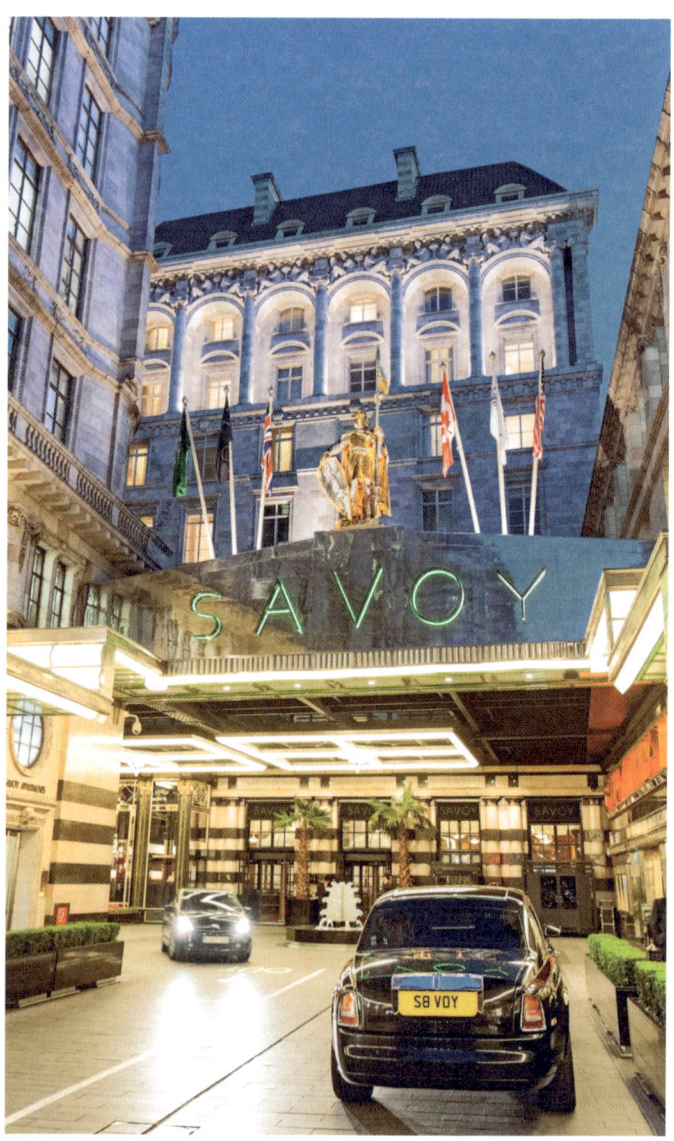

THE SAVOY

Opened in 1889, The Savoy was London's first luxury hotel. Much like Taylor, it didn't shy away from trying new things. In fact, it was one of the first to introduce electric lifts in the city (even if it did take nine minutes to get to the top floor). It was at The Savoy's plush black and gold Beaufort Bar that Taylor posed for her *Vanity Fair* photoshoot in 2015, wearing her trademark red lipstick and an array of designer outfits. The singer later revisited the hotel to film parts of the "End Game" music video, hiring out the lavish Royal Suite. The fifth-floor apartment offers expansive panoramic views of the River Thames as well as London landmarks such as the London Eye. Want to book a stay? You better start saving. Rates for the Royal Suite begin at £17,500 a night…

———

📍 D1 · 🏠 Strand, WC2R 0EZ
🚇 Charing Cross, Waterloo · Ⓜ Embankment, Temple
🕐 Daily, for hotel residents · Ⓦ thesavoylondon.com

KING'S COLLEGE LONDON

If Taylor had a song about touring in her teenage years, King's College London would almost definitely get mentioned. One of Taylor's earliest London live shows was held here, at the world-class university's student nightclub in 2008. Unfortunately, the club closed in 2013 due to financial issues but you can still take a guided tour of the university itself (it was founded back in 1829, so you better believe there are stories to tell). King's College graduates still reminisce about the intimate gig, which was a far cry from the sold-out stadiums that Taylor is known for today.

———————————

♀ C2 · 🏠 Surrey Street, WC2R 2NS
🚇 Temple · Ⓦ kcl.ac.uk

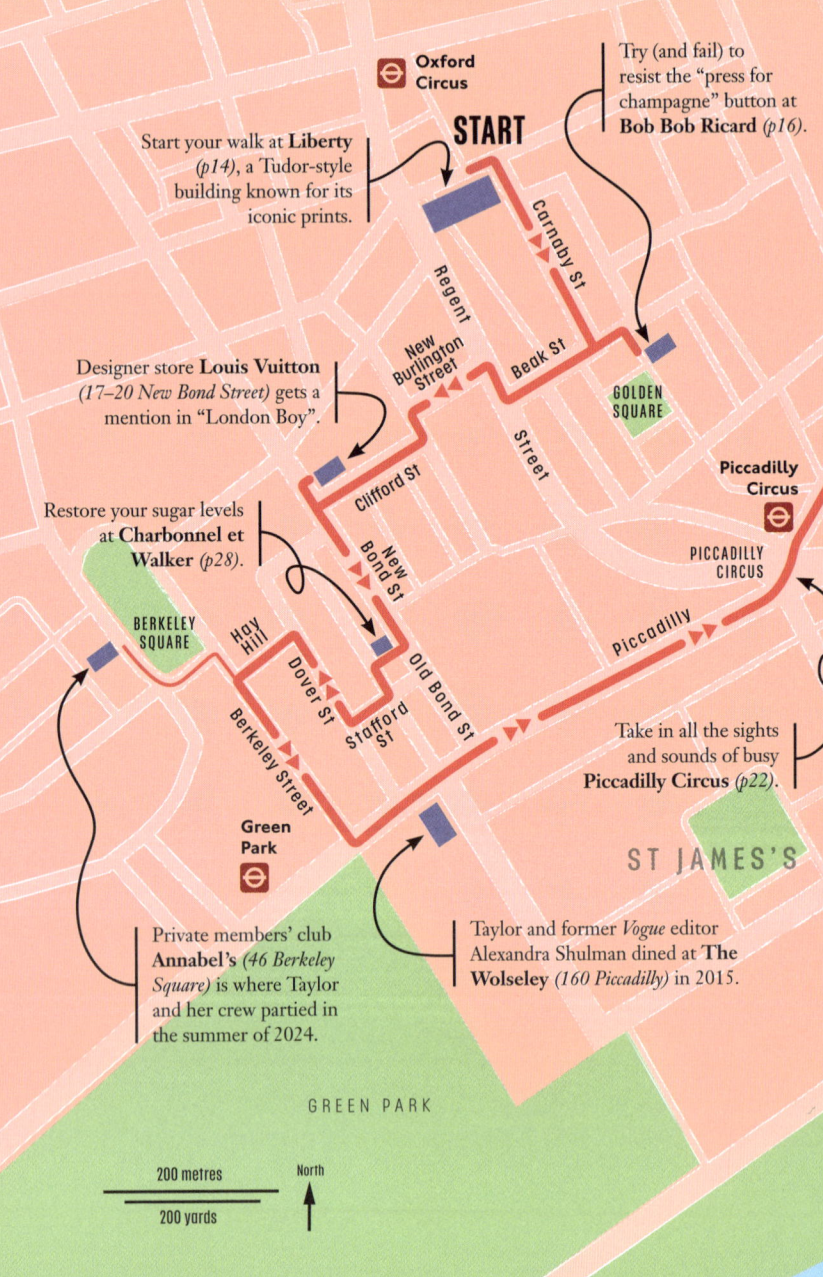

Oxford Circus

Start your walk at **Liberty** *(p14)*, a Tudor-style building known for its iconic prints.

START

Try (and fail) to resist the "press for champagne" button at **Bob Bob Ricard** *(p16)*.

Designer store **Louis Vuitton** *(17–20 New Bond Street)* gets a mention in "London Boy".

Restore your sugar levels at **Charbonnel et Walker** *(p28)*.

Regent Street

New Burlington Street

Carnaby St

Beak St

GOLDEN SQUARE

Clifford St

New Bond St

Piccadilly Circus

PICCADILLY CIRCUS

Piccadilly

Take in all the sights and sounds of busy **Piccadilly Circus** *(p22)*.

BERKELEY SQUARE

Hay Hill

Dover St

Stafford St

Old Bond St

Berkeley Street

Green Park

ST JAMES'S

Private members' club **Annabel's** *(46 Berkeley Square)* is where Taylor and her crew partied in the summer of 2024.

Taylor and former *Vogue* editor Alexandra Shulman dined at **The Wolseley** *(160 Piccadilly)* in 2015.

GREEN PARK

200 metres

200 yards

North

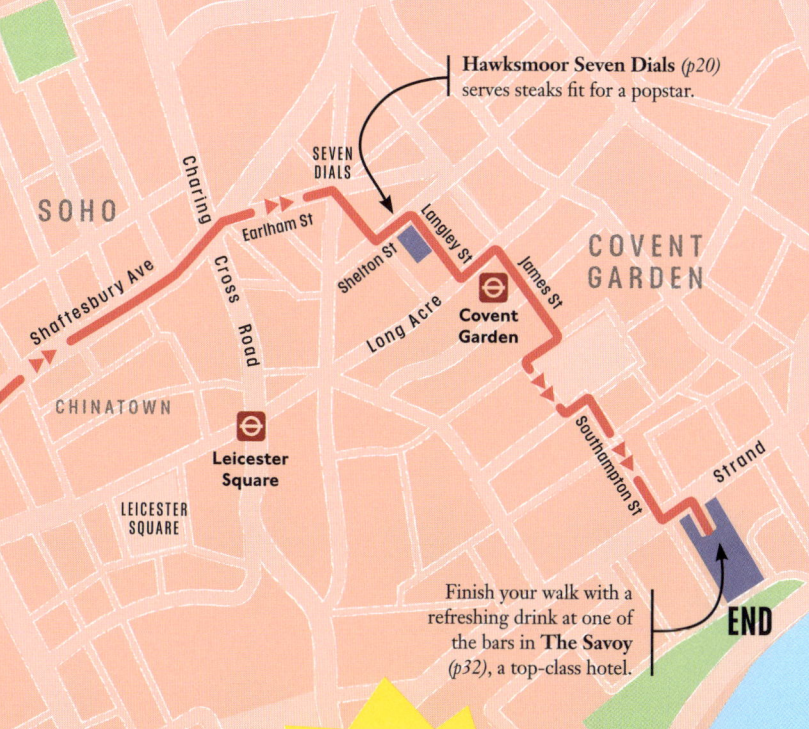

Hawksmoor Seven Dials (*p20*)
serves steaks fit for a popstar.

SEVEN
DIALS

SOHO

Charing

Earlham St

Cross Road

Shelton St

Langley St

Long Acre

COVENT
GARDEN

Covent
Garden

James St

Shaftesbury Ave

CHINATOWN

Leicester
Square

Southampton St

Strand

LEICESTER
SQUARE

END

Finish your walk with a
refreshing drink at one of
the bars in **The Savoy**
(*p32*), a top-class hotel.

WALKING TOUR
CENTRAL LONDON

Distance 3 km (2 miles)
Nearest Tube to Starting Point Oxford Circus

Even superstars can come across like tourists in London.
And why not? Most of us want to visit top attractions, dine
at the coolest restaurants and splurge a little while on a
city break. This short walk takes you past locations
Taylor's visited in person, as well as places featured in her
music videos and songs. And there's still plenty to see and
enjoy if you don't want to break the bank, from pretty
Carnaby Street to vibrant Piccadilly Circus.

LORD'S CRICKET GROUND

Cricket and Taylor. The two wouldn't normally be associated with one another. But believe it or not, the award-winning singer visited Lord's Cricket Ground, also known as Lord's, with radio DJ Greg James in 2014. The two enjoyed a spot of carpool karaoke in north London first, singing Taylor's newly released single at the time: "Blank Space". (The YouTube video has since garnered more than 20 million views.) As they were in the area already, cricket enthusiast James suggested a quick photo at the historic grounds, which were set up in 1814 by professional cricketer Thomas Lord. Today, the iconic sporting venue can be visited on guided tours, or with a ticket to a live game. It's unlikely you'll run into Taylor here, though (you might have better luck at an NFL game).

📍 B1 • 🏠 St John's Road, NW8 8QN
🚆 Marylebone • Ⓤ St John's Wood; check website on match days
Ⓦ lords.org

ABBEY ROAD STUDIOS

The world's first recording studio, the iconic Abbey Road is often associated with The Beatles. But for die-hard Taylor fans, it's a spot that the singer has visited on more than one occasion, most notably in 2021 to re-record her Christmas song "Christmas Tree Farm (Old Timey Version)" with an impressive 70-piece orchestra. And while the working studio is largely off limits to the public, there's still plenty for the average visitor to see and do here. Stroll over the famous pedestrian crossing out front, write on the graffiti wall and purchase some merchandise at the official Abbey Road shop. Oh, and make sure to look on the studio's website afterwards – you might just make an appearance on the Crossing Cam hall of fame… so make that strut count.

———————

📍 B1 • 🏠 3 Abbey Road, NW8 9AY
🚆 Kilburn High Road, South Hampstead • Ⓤ St John's Wood
🕐 Studio: closed to the public; shop: 9:30am–5:30pm Mon–Sat,
10am–5pm Sun • Ⓦ abbeyroad.com

LONDON ZOO

A self-proclaimed cat lover, Taylor's appreciation for felines is unmatched – not many celebrities would pose with their furry pet for the *TIME* Person of the Year cover. That said, Taylor appears to adore all animals, and she is certainly no stranger to visiting the zoo on a day off. In 2012, wrapped up in a maroon duffel coat and donning a pair of brogues, Taylor was snapped making some feathered friends at London Zoo. This famous city attraction marked her visit 12 years later by offering 25 per cent off the admission fee to her concert goers. Though small by international standards, the zoo is home to more than 750 animal species and around 15,000 creatures in total. The largest enclosure, the Land of the Lions, is particularly impressive. Watch Asiatic lions prowl around the zoo's rendering of the Gir Forest in western India, or book a memorable stay at the London Zoo Lodge to stay within roaring distance of these big cats.

📍 B1 • ♠ Outer Circle, Regent's Park, NW1 4RY
🚇 Camden Road • Ⓜ Camden Town, Chalk Farm
🕐 Hours vary, check website • Ⓦ londonzoo.org

PRIMROSE HILL

Taylor and Joe Alwyn might have called Primrose Hill home during the COVID-19 pandemic, but it's another resident altogether that's put this leafy North London area on the map: Paddington. Set-jetters regularly rock up to photograph the pastel-painted townhouses featured in the tales of everyone's favourite marmalade sandwich-loving bear, much to the real homeowners' dismay. We say give the streets a wide berth and head to Primrose Hill itself. Once a venue for duels, it's now better known for serving up spectacular views of the London skyline – and it's just a short walk to Camden Market *(p48)* and London Zoo *(p42)*, too.

📍 B1 • 🏠 NW8 • 🚇 Kentish Town • Ⓜ Chalk Farm
🕐 Daily • Ⓦ royalparks.org.uk

CAMDEN MARKET

Whether you're here for a morning browse or an afternoon stroll like Taylor in her song "London Boy", Camden Market has something for everyone. Its name is slightly misleading, as it's not just one market; Camden Market is actually a warren of interconnected markets running along Chalk Farm Road and Camden High Street. Stalls are laden with vintage clothes and jewellery, plus quirky handmade crafts. Feeling peckish? Delicious and boundary-pushing street food can be found here too, like Yorkshire Burritos. And then there's the musical heritage. Famous venues like the Roundhouse were at the heart of Britain's counterculture in the 1960s and 70s, hosting the likes of Blondie and Jimi Hendrix. Stables Market is also home to the bronze statue of late singer Amy Winehouse, who used to live near here. The North Londoner won a Grammy for Best New Artist in 2008, beating a young Taylor to the award.

📍 C1 · 🏠 Camden Lock Place, NW1 8AF
🚆 Camden Road · Ⓜ Camden Town
🕐 Hours vary, check website · Ⓦ camdenmarket.com

KENTISH DELIGHT

This small takeaway might not look like anything special from the outside but you'd be foolish to skip it. Why? It's rumoured to be Taylor's favourite kebab shop. Introduced to this modest North London takeaway by Joe Alwyn, Taylor has been putting this place on the map since 2017, when she featured it in the "End Game" music video. But while her relationship with Joe ended, her love affair with Kentish Delight did not. Taylor reportedly placed a large order for her crew while touring London in summer 2024. What's Taylor's go-to order? According to the owner, it's a chicken doner kebab. Perhaps unsurprisingly, the staff are loyal fans – you only need look at the decor. The shop's walls and windows are plastered with behind-the-scenes images from the music video and a framed selfie with the star.

C1 · 🏠 381 Kentish Town Road, NW5 2TJ
🚇 Kentish Town · 🚆 Kentish Town
🕐 Midday–midnight Mon–Thu, midday–1am Fri–Sat,
3pm–midnight Sunday · 📞 020 7998 1446

BULL & GATE

Prior to its makeover in 2015, this Victorian watering hole used to host major indie bands, including Coldplay, Blur and Oasis. More recently it featured in Taylor's "End Game" music video, where she raises a glass with pals in the swanky Boulogne Bar, a private area on the first floor. Today, there's still a lot to love about the Bull & Gate pub. This charming North London venue hosts regular quiz nights, stocks communal board games and shows live sport. And it's cosy, especially in autumn, when there's a roaring log fire. Top tip: the pub is a short walk from the O2 Kentish Town venue, making it *the* place to go for a pre- or post-concert drink with friends.

📍 C1 • 🏠 389 Kentish Town Road, NW5 2TJ
🚆 Kentish Town • Ⓜ Kentish Town • 🕐 11am–11pm Mon–Thu,
11am–midnight Fri–Sat, midday–10:30pm Sun
Ⓦ bullandgatenw5.co.uk

NORTH LONDON

Distance 5 km (3 miles) **Nearest Tube to Starting Point** St John's Wood

Ditch the Taylor treadmill strut for a stroll outside in pretty North London, the singer's former stomping ground. Home to countless green spaces, famous attractions like London Zoo and cultural gems like Lord's Cricket Ground, this area is where Taylor's popped up the most. This guided walk will take you past some of the sights she's visited over the years and we've snuck in some great photo-worthy locations, too.

ST JOHN'S WOOD

St John's Wood

Abbey Road

Start your walk at **Abbey Road Studios** *(p40)* and scrawl your favourite Taylor lyrics on the graffiti wall.

Walk past the majestic **Lord's Cricket Ground** *(p38)* or book tickets to see a match.

START

Grove End Road

St John's Wood Road

Prince Albert Road

Regent's Canal

Outer Circle

Snap photos of the ever evolving London skyline at **Primrose Hill** *(p44)*.

Chalk Farm

Chalk Farm Road

Finish your walk at **Camden Market** *(p48)* with a photo at "umbrella alley".

END

Taylor visited the **Roundhouse** *(Chalk Farm Road)*, a music venue, in 2015 to support model Karlie Kloss's charity fundraiser.

Park Rd

Regent's

Regent's Canal

Is Taylor a modern-day Sylvia Plath? Decide at Plath's historic blue plaque *(3 Chalcot Square)*.

Camden Town

PRIMROSE HILL

Prince Albert Road

CAMDEN

Outer Circle

After a stroll beside the Regent's Canal, visit the big cats at **London Zoo** *(p42)*.

THE REGENT'S PARK

200 metres

200 yards

North

THE GARDEN GATE

Taylor is well known (and admired) for including both literal and metaphorical lyrics in her songs. Indeed, her recordings often spur fans to post their own theories and interpretations about her lyrics online. Take the 2019 hit song "Cruel Summer", which seems to reference this North London pub. For the diehard Swift fan, it's not hard to imagine her sneaking in here – the Hampstead boozer is located right in the heart of her old stomping ground, and it's arguably got one of the best pub gardens in London. What better place to spend a mild summer evening (cruel or otherwise)?

———————

♀ B1 · ♠ 14 South End Road, NW3 2QE
🚇 Hampstead Heath · 🚇 Belsize Park
🕐 Hours vary, check website · Ⓦ thegardengatehampstead.co.uk

THE HOLLY BUSH

Tucked away from Hampstead's main high street (but no less popular for it), The Holly Bush has proper warm English pub vibes. Taylor was spotted here back in 2013 with actor Douglas Booth, the pair reportedly introduced to each other by Booth's co-star in *Romeo & Juliet*, Hailee Steinfeld. And, much like most Shakespearean love stories, this one didn't seem to have a happy ending. But fizzling romance aside, this place? Gorgeous. Inside, the 18th-century wood-panelled pub is all log fires and cosy corners, while outside the pretty cream-coloured exterior is often decorated with flower baskets. It's basically begging to be photographed. As for the food and drink – delicious. Inevitably it's a hit with dog-walkers fresh off a stroll on nearby Hampstead Heath *(p60)*, and who can blame them.

📍 B1 · 🏠 22 Hollymount, NW3 6SG
🚇 Hampstead · 🕐 Midday–11pm Mon–Sat, midday–10:30pm Sun
ⓦ hollybushhampstead.co.uk

HAMPSTEAD HEATH

Ancient woodlands, willowy ponds and sprawling grasslands: Hampstead Heath is a favourite green space among restless Londoners in search of escape. And you could spend days walking here – it's the largest of inner London's parklands, spanning around 320 hectares (790 acres). The green space seemed to make an impression on Taylor, who referenced the Heath in two of her songs ("So Long, London" and "London Boy"). Wander for long enough and you'll stumble upon gems like Parliament Hill, which provides a breathtaking view of the city, or Hill Garden, a charming Edwardian garden with a raised pergola walkway. Hampstead Heath is especially beautiful in spring when the flowers are in full bloom, and when warmer weather allows for wild swimming in the natural ponds.

———————

📍 B1 • 🏠 NW3
🚇 Hampstead Heath, Gospel Oak • 🚇 Hampstead
Ⓦ cityoflondon.gov.uk

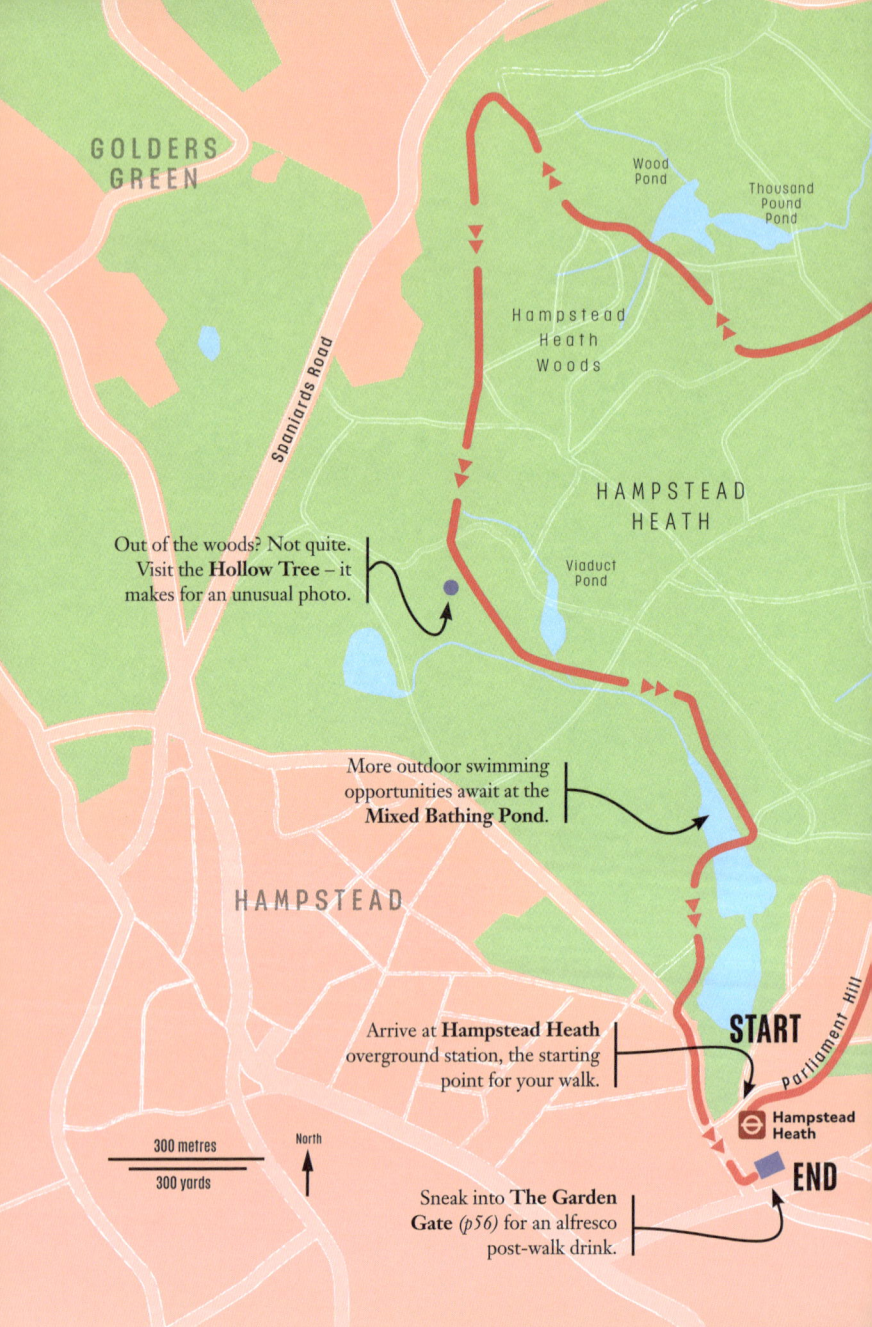

GOLDERS
GREEN

Wood
Pond

Thousand
Pound
Pond

Spaniards Road

Hampstead
Heath
Woods

HAMPSTEAD
HEATH

Out of the woods? Not quite.
Visit the **Hollow Tree** – it
makes for an unusual photo.

Viaduct
Pond

More outdoor swimming
opportunities await at the
Mixed Bathing Pond.

HAMPSTEAD

START

Arrive at **Hampstead Heath**
overground station, the starting
point for your walk.

Parliament Hill

⊖ Hampstead
Heath

300 metres

North

END

300 yards

Sneak into **The Garden
Gate** (*p56*) for an alfresco
post-walk drink.

Stock
Pond

Turns out Londoners can have nice things, including **Kenwood Ladies' Bathing Pond**.

Bird
Sanctuary
Pond

Taylor's ex Harry Styles is a Hampstead resident. He's been snapped cooling off at **Highgate Men's Bathing Pond**.

Highgate
Pond

Walk to **Parliament Hill** *(p60)* – the panoramic views are beyond anyone's wildest dreams.

WALKING TOUR

HAMPSTEAD HEATH

Distance 6.5 km (4 miles) **Nearest Overground to Starting Point** Hampstead Heath

This charming walk will have you wondering if you're still in London. A short distance from the heart of city sits Hampstead Heath, a green oasis that borders Hampstead and Highgate. Get your heart rate up with a walk to scenic viewpoints or a swim at the bathing ponds, and finish off at the pub.

HIGHGATE

Nestled between Hampstead and Muswell Hill, the uber-exclusive Highgate is best known for its cute woodlands, cosy cafés and impressive cemetery. But for Taylor fans, it has other accolades: it's just a stone's throw from where Joe Alwyn grew up *and* it gets a short-but-sweet mention in "London Boy". Its legendary graveyard isn't one to skip. No, you won't find a headstone for Taylor's reputation here, but you will find some seriously big names. Built in the 19th century, Highgate Cemetery is the resting place of singer George Michael, philosopher Karl Marx, and poet and novelist George Eliot, whose real name was Mary Ann Evans (because in the 1800s, women had to use pseudonyms to get ahead). And talking of noms de plume, Taylor and Joe know a thing about those. Taylor is credited as writer Nils Sjöberg on Calvin Harris's song "This Is What You Came For", while Joe is listed on some of Taylor's tracks as William Bowery.

📍 B1 · 🚌 N10; Highgate Cemetery: Swain's Lane, N6 6PJ
🚇 Upper Holloway · Ⓡ Highgate, Archway
🕐 Cemetery: 10am–5pm daily (Nov–Feb: to 4pm) · ⓦ highgatecemetery.org

THE FLASK

Just a short walk from Highgate Cemetery (*p66*) is The Flask, a historic pub and restaurant. Needless to say, its proximity to the graveyard has led to rumours that it's haunted, with guests recalling seeing the ghost of a man in a Cavalier uniform at the bar, plus a Spanish barmaid. Today, the scariest thing is probably the price of a pint of beer, but hey, that's not specific to The Flask. All horror aside, the gastro pub is also known for its literary links, with Byron, Shelley and Keats regulars here at one time or another. Today, The Flask's patioed pub garden and Sunday roasts get rave reviews from locals, who make their way up the steep Highgate Village to pull up a chair – which is exactly what Taylor and Joe Alwyn did in 2018.

———————

📍 B1 • 🏠 77 Highgate West Hill, N6 6BU • 🚇 Highgate
🕐 11am–11pm Mon–Sat, midday–10:30pm Sun • ⓦ theflaskhighgate.com

CROUCH END

The kind of place where everyone has a cute dog, a reusable coffee cup and a strong opinion on what makes the perfect brunch spot, Crouch End is frequently voted the best place to live in London. It's a little off the beaten Tube map (there's no Tube station here, so you might need to embrace the London bus system like a true local), but you'll know you've made it when you see the Crouch End Clock Tower, a red-brick landmark. During the lockdown era, the neighbourhood was reportedly one of Taylor's low-key London hideouts, while visiting then Crouch End resident, Joe Alwyn. Taylor isn't the only music royalty to spend time here, by the way. Church Studios, an iconic recording spot, has hosted legends like Florence + The Machine and Patti Smith, both of whom (as you well know) made their mark on *The Tortured Poets Department*.

♀ C1 • 🏠 N8 • 🚇 Crouch Hill

SHOREDITCH

What's classified as cool in London changes faster than Taylor switching outfits on the Eras Tour, but Shoreditch just about clings on to its cool kid credentials. Referenced in "London Boy", this East London hangout is edgy and eclectic, known for its indie markets, great food and craft breweries. And then there's the street art. There's tons of it here; in fact, in the run-up to Taylor's massive Wembley Stadium shows in 2024, a fan-made mural on Redchurch Street became a pilgrimage spot for fans. If you missed it, don't worry. Shoreditch loves a Taylor moment (check out the stalls stocking Taylor-inspired jackets at Spitalfields Market), so there's a good chance another will pop up soon.

📍 C1 · 🏠 E2
🚇 Old Street, Shoreditch High Street, Liverpool Street
Ⓡ Old Street, Liverpool Street

It's not wonderland but it's pretty close. Sip on drinks at **Looking Glass Cocktail Club** *(49 Hackney Road)*, an Alice in Wonderland-themed speakeasy.

Hackney Road

SHOREDITCH

Shoreditch High Street

Trendy **Redchurch Street**, lined with fashionable boutiques, once had a fan-made Taylor mural.

Redchurch Street

If Taylor's got you into American football, watch a game on screen at **Boxpark Shoreditch** *(2-10 Bethnal Green Road)*, your final stop.

END

Shoreditch High Street

Sclater Street

Shoreditch High Street

Commercial Street

SPITALFIELDS

100 metres
100 yards

North

Start your walk at **Rough Trade East** *(Old Truman Brewery, 91 Brick Lane)* and browse Taylor's vinyls.

START

Dray Walk

Tortured poets can buy their own typewriters at the **Typewriter Emporium and Vintage Shop** *(146 Brick Lane)*.

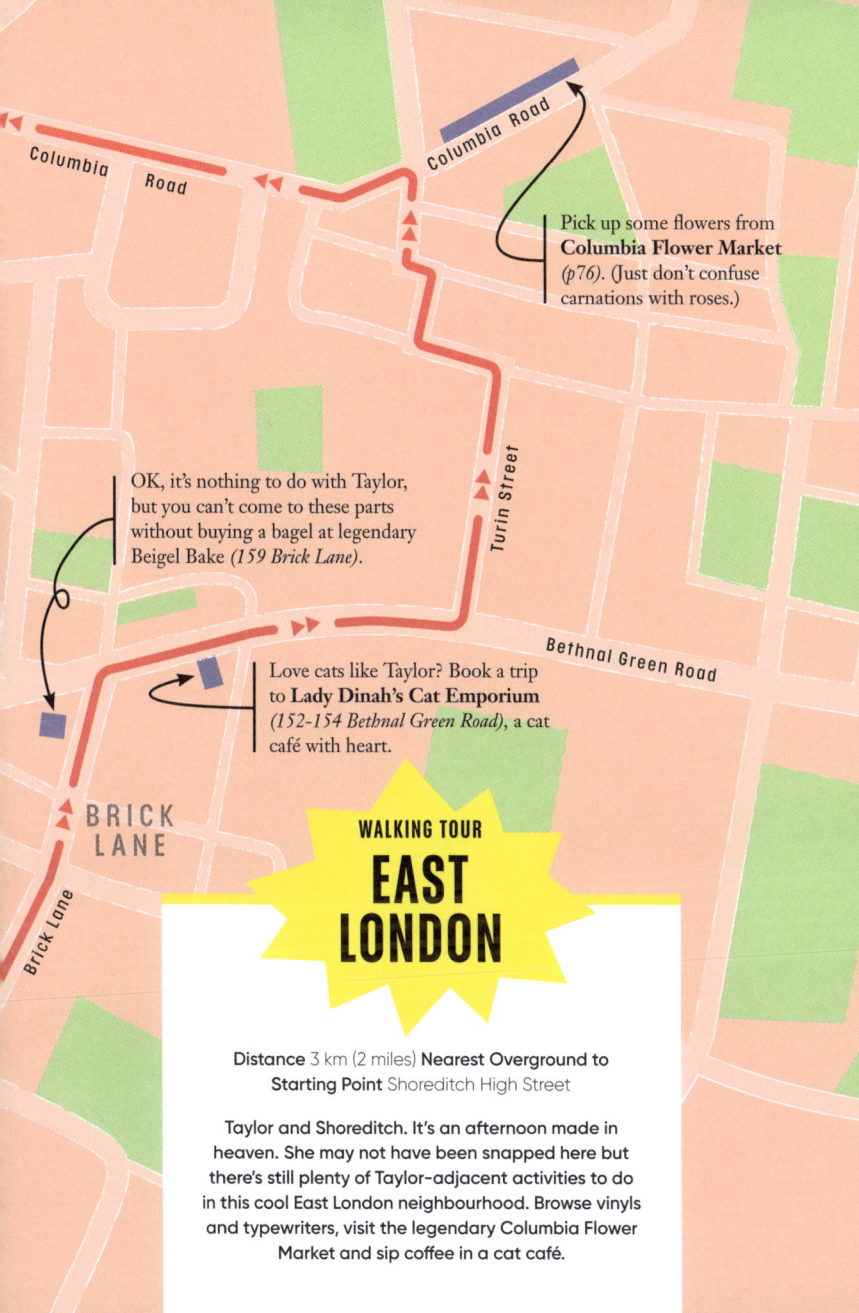

Columbia Road

Columbia Road

Pick up some flowers from **Columbia Flower Market** *(p76)*. (Just don't confuse carnations with roses.)

Turin Street

OK, it's nothing to do with Taylor, but you can't come to these parts without buying a bagel at legendary Beigel Bake *(159 Brick Lane)*.

Bethnal Green Road

Love cats like Taylor? Book a trip to **Lady Dinah's Cat Emporium** *(152-154 Bethnal Green Road)*, a cat café with heart.

BRICK LANE

Brick Lane

WALKING TOUR

EAST LONDON

Distance 3 km (2 miles) **Nearest Overground to Starting Point** Shoreditch High Street

Taylor and Shoreditch. It's an afternoon made in heaven. She may not have been snapped here but there's still plenty of Taylor-adjacent activities to do in this cool East London neighbourhood. Browse vinyls and typewriters, visit the legendary Columbia Flower Market and sip coffee in a cat café.

HACKNEY

Ah Hackney, another East London cool kid. Here you'll find Columbia Road Flower Market, where fresh blooms line the street; London Fields Lido, an Olympic-sized outdoor swimming pool just waiting for you to recreate Taylor's famous stage dive; and 58 – yes, 58 – parks, perfect for a wander. Grey skies and rain clouds threatening the fun? Channel the "Blank Space" music video and head to one of Hackney's many mini indoor golf courses. Look, Hackney just doesn't try that hard and that's why we love it. It's no wonder Taylor name-drops it on "London Boy" (maybe she heard about it from her *Cats* co-star Idris Elba, too; the certified Hackney legend kicks off the track with his unmistakable London accent).

♀ D1 · ♠ E1
🚇 Hackney Central, Hackney Downs

THE FLORIST ARMS

Coated in dark green paint and bedecked with tumbling plants, this classic East London boozer is the ultimate hidden gem. Unfortunately for Taylor it wasn't hidden away enough and she was snapped leaving the pub with singer Tom Odell in 2013. The blonde-haired duo, who had previously bonded over Tom's cover of "I Knew You Were Trouble", had both been in attendance at the 2013 Brit Awards earlier that week. Tom may have walked away with the prestigious Critics' Choice Award but you certainly don't have to be an award-winning singer to enjoy a pint here. Friendly staff are on hand to serve local and international beers as well as delicious sourdough pizzas. The interiors are particularly festive in December, when the bar is draped with bunting and twinkling lights.

♀ D1 · 🏠 255 Globe Road, E2 0JD
🚇 Cambridge Heath · 🚇 Bethnal Green
🕐 Hours vary, check website · ⓦ floristarms.co.uk

THE O2

Naturally Taylor has followed in the footsteps of the world's biggest music names by performing in London's largest indoor concert venue, the O2. The 20,000-seat arena played host to the pop phenomenon during her Speak Now and Red tours, plus various Capital FM Jingle Bell Balls. Taylor also made surprise appearances on stage for other acts, including bands Haim and The 1975, though Taylor herself upscaled to Wembley Stadium *(p112)* for her Eras Tour, which can host nearly 90,000 fans. While the O2 might not top your sightseeing list, it's a fantastic place to watch live entertainment, catch up with friends over dinner or indulge in a spot of shopping, with both a food court and mall to explore. Thrill-seekers can also follow in the footsteps of singers George Ezra and Billie Eilish by climbing 52 m (170 ft) up the O2 for epic views of London. Alternatively, take the IFS Cloud Cable Car here to soak up views of the city.

📍 D2 · 🏠 Peninsula Square, SE10 0DX
🚇 North Greenwich · 🚌 North Greenwich
🕐 Hours vary, check website · Ⓦ theo2.co.uk

THE THAMES

There are few things better than cruising along the River Thames on a fine summer's evening. And Taylor would know, for that is exactly what she did with a close group of pals in 2015. Perched on the stern, Taylor shared a photo featuring DJ Calvin Harris (who she was dating at the time), singer Joe Jonas, and models Gigi Hadid and Karlie Kloss. While the singer-songwriter hired a private charter for the sunset voyage, there are plenty of ways to travel along the river without breaking the bank. Hop on an Uber Boat by Thames Clippers, race along the water in a speedboat or enjoy a guided tour with a glass of fizz. However you do it, you'll see key London sights like the Houses of Parliament and Tower Bridge as you ride the waves.

📍 C2 · Ⓦ thamesclippers.com

MILLENNIUM BRIDGE

Affectionately known as the "wobbly bridge" by Londoners due to its initial swaying on opening day, the Millennium Bridge makes a brief but memorable cameo in Taylor's "End Game" music video. Wearing a sparkly sequinned dress and a fluffy blue coat, Taylor walks across the illuminated bridge after dark. Used by locals and tourists alike, the Millennium Bridge is thought to carry thousands of foot passengers across the snaking Thames river each day. It connects St Paul's Cathedral on the north bank with the striking Tate Modern art gallery and renowned Shakespeare's Globe on the south. A key river crossing, the 325-m- (1,066-ft-) long bridge also features in movies such as *Harry Potter and the Half-Blood Prince*, giving rise to a second nickname: the Harry Potter Bridge. The only thing better than this bridge is one from Taylor's discography.

📍 C2 • 🏠 Thames Embankment, EC4V 3QH
🚇 Blackfriars • 🚇 Blackfriars • ⚓ Bankside Pier

SOUTH BANK

Hugging the winding River Thames, South Bank is home to cultural institutions like the National Theatre as well as the striking London Eye, a 135-m- (443-ft-) high observation wheel. As it's beautifully illuminated at night, it's no wonder the director of the "End Game" music video chose to shoot South Bank (albeit briefly) as the backdrop for Taylor's bus journey across the city. The area also has strong links to film, which Taylor has been experimenting with herself. She directed *All Too Well: The Short Film*, which won a Grammy in 2023 for Best Music Video. What does this mean for fans? Should Taylor release any more short films or concert documentaries, South Bank is the place to go. Its IMAX cinema, located near Waterloo station, has the UK's biggest screen and was in high demand during the release of *Taylor Swift: The Eras Tour* (2023).

———————

📍 C2 · 🏠 BFI IMAX: 1 Charlie Chaplin Walk, South Bank, SE1 8XR
🚇 Waterloo · 🚆 Waterloo · ⓦ whatson.bfi.org.uk/imax

THE BLACK DOG

Widely regarded to be the pub name-dropped in *The Tortured Poets Department*, the Black Dog is the perfect South London spot to enjoy a swift pint and a traditional roast dinner. Fans have flocked to Vauxhall to visit the award-winning tavern but it's easy to see why it was a favourite with Londoners to begin with. Based in a historic building, behind a railway line and alongside the verdant Vauxhall pleasure gardens, the Black Dog has always been a go-to place for post-work drinks and relaxed dinners with friends. Expect striped awnings, hanging baskets laden with flowers and Taylor's lyrics scrawled on a blackboard. Inside, dark wooden floors lead to quiet corners and a small walled garden area, ideal for summer evenings. Come for themed merch or a relaxed catch up with pals – just don't forget to turn off your friend-tracking devices.

---

9 C2 · ♠ 112 Vauxhall Walk, SE11 5ER · 🚇 Vauxhall · 🚉 Vauxhall
🕐 Noon–11pm Mon-Sat, noon–10pm Sun
ⓦ theblackdogvauxhall.co.uk

BRIXTON

Another much-loved neighbourhood name-checked in "London Boy", Brixton is pure vibes. There's the Ritzy cinema with its retro listings board; two pretty epic covered markets, full of great places to eat, drink and shop; and Pop Brixton, a split-level street-food market fashioned out of shipping containers. And from Pop Brixton to pop royalty: Taylor rocked up to the O2 Academy Brixton in 2020 to collect her second NME award. That's just one of quite a few music venues in these parts, incidentally, so if you're all about seeing stars on the stage, or perhaps want to catch the next big thing, this is the place to be. Not sure where to start? Try Brixton Jamm. This independent music venue once platformed Adele. It's also a short distance from where music legend David Bowie was born, if you fancy taking a ziggy-zag walk through Brixton.

📍 C2 · 🏠 SW9 · 🚇 Brixton · 🚇 Brixton

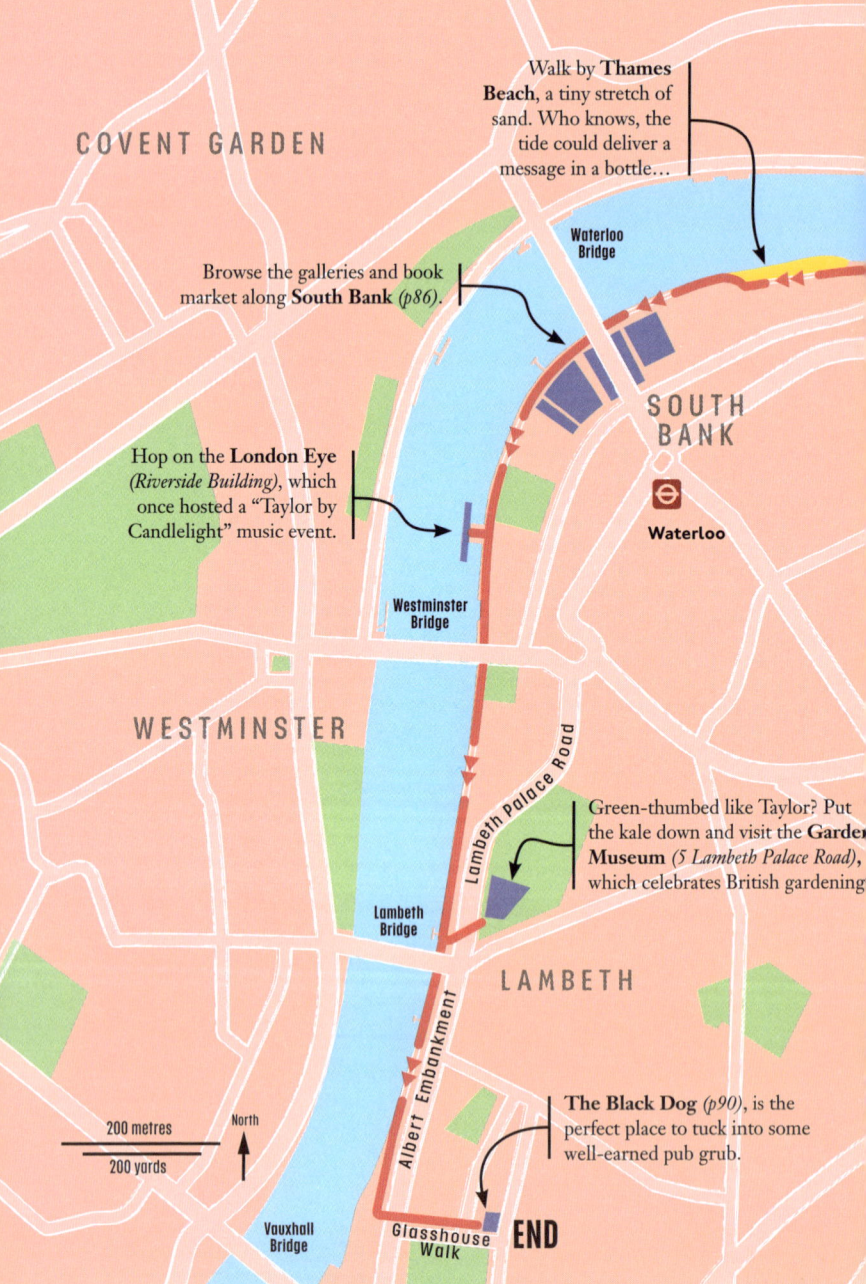

COVENT GARDEN

Walk by **Thames Beach**, a tiny stretch of sand. Who knows, the tide could deliver a message in a bottle…

Waterloo Bridge

Browse the galleries and book market along **South Bank** *(p86)*.

SOUTH BANK

Waterloo

Hop on the **London Eye** *(Riverside Building)*, which once hosted a "Taylor by Candlelight" music event.

Westminster Bridge

WESTMINSTER

Lambeth Palace Road

Green-thumbed like Taylor? Put the kale down and visit the **Garden Museum** *(5 Lambeth Palace Road)*, which celebrates British gardening

Lambeth Bridge

LAMBETH

Albert Embankment

The **Black Dog** *(p90)*, is the perfect place to tuck into some well-earned pub grub.

200 metres
200 yards

North

Vauxhall Bridge

Glasshouse Walk

END

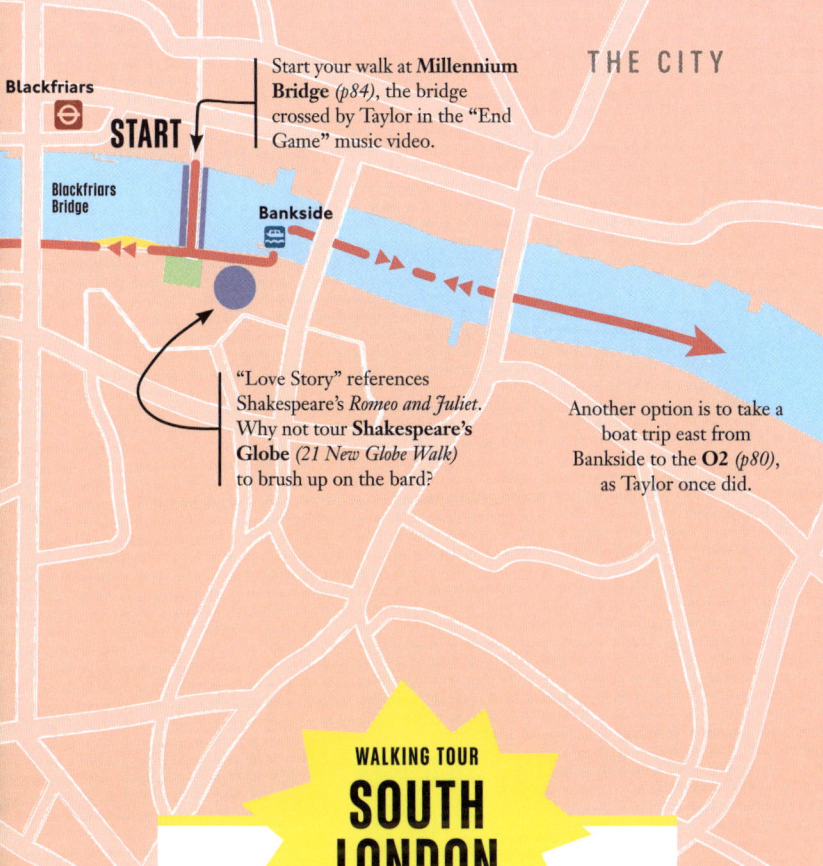

Blackfriars

START

Blackfriars Bridge

Bankside

Start your walk at **Millennium Bridge** *(p84)*, the bridge crossed by Taylor in the "End Game" music video.

"Love Story" references Shakespeare's *Romeo and Juliet*. Why not tour **Shakespeare's Globe** *(21 New Globe Walk)* to brush up on the bard?

Another option is to take a boat trip east from Bankside to the **O2** *(p80)*, as Taylor once did.

WALKING TOUR
SOUTH LONDON

Distance 4 km (2.5 miles) **Nearest Tube to Starting Point** Blackfriars

Taylor's sparkly boots haven't strutted around South London much but there's still plenty to explore, including legendary theatres, cool galleries and views of London's top sights. This walk along the Thames follows (briefly) in Taylor's actual footsteps, crossing the Millennium Bridge, then tracking west along the south bank. Bring your camera – you'll want to remember this one.

BENIHANA CHELSEA

This unassuming spot might not scream drama, but step inside (and down 32 steps, so choose your shoes wisely) and you're in for a show. Japanese-style Benihana is all about culinary performance, where ordering teppanyaki means scoring front-row seats to flames, flips and foodie theatrics. For someone who's usually on stage, it must have been a treat being in the audience for Taylor, who visited in 2011. Not a fan of Japanese food? No problem. You're on King's Road, aka fashion paradise. Swing by World's End *(430 King's Road)*, the quirky store of late designer Vivienne Westwood, for another Taylor hit: the pop star has rocked Westwood's designs both on tour and out for dinner.

♀ B2 • 🏠 77 King's Road, SW3 4NX
🚇 Sloane Square • ⚓ Cadogan Pier
🕐 Midday–3pm & 5pm–late Mon–Fri; midday–late Sat & Sun (last table
reservation: 10pm) • Ⓦ benihanainternational.com

VICTORIA AND ALBERT MUSEUM

The Victoria and Albert Museum (V&A) was on every fan's radar during the summer of 2024 when it briefly became the home of the Taylor-themed exhibition: "Taylor Swift: Songbook Trail". The temporary installation snaked across the museum, with each stop exploring a different chapter of the singer-songwriter's life, from her childhood in Pennsylvania to adulthood as a re-recording artist. Items on display included personalized blue cowboy boots worn by Swift at the Soul2Soul II Tour in 2007, a serpent-themed microphone used on the 2018 Reputation tour and a Victorian-themed mourning dress worn by Taylor in the award-winning "Fortnight" music video. For some, the V&A may feel empty without Taylor's 13 exhibits but that's certainly not the case. This treasure of a museum has one of the world's biggest collections of art and design. Visiting on the last Friday of the month? Make the most of Friday Late – a free evening event that celebrates contemporary art and emerging artists.

———————

📍 B2 • 🏠 Cromwell Road, SW7 2RL • Ⓜ South Kensington
🕐 10am–5:45pm daily (Friday: 10am–10pm) • Ⓦ vam.ac.uk

HYDE PARK

Taylor was almost unrecognizable on her solo visit to Hyde Park in 2012. Tucked under an umbrella, headphones in and without a microphone in sight, she had free rein to snap photos of swans and visit the Princess Diana Memorial Fountain. It's safe to say her visits have been a little less low-key since then. The US star performed here in 2015 for British Summer Time (BST) Hyde Park, singing synthy pop hits while introducing the crowd to her then girl squad: models Kendall Jenner, Martha Hunt, Karlie Kloss, Gigi Hadid and Cara Delevingne, and tennis pro Serena Williams. In 2020, Taylor returned to the Royal Park, this time as a headline act for the festival. Today, the chances of seeing Taylor on a walk here are pretty slim but that doesn't mean the park should be skipped. A green sanctuary in the "big smoke", Hyde Park has endless paths to explore. You could stumble across Speaker's Corner, a marker of free speech, or the Serpentine Lido, a popular spot for boating and wild swimming.

📍 B2 · 🏠 W2 · 🚇 Hyde Park Corner, Marble Arch
🕐 Hours vary, check website · Ⓦ royalparks.org.uk

KENSINGTON PALACE

Kensington Palace is a beautiful escape from the busy city and a wonderful place to immerse yourself in British royal history. Glide down the King's Staircase, admire Queen Mary II's grand bedroom and smell the flowers in the Diana Princess of Wales Sunken Garden. And speaking of princesses... Taylor attended the Winter Whites Gala charity event at Kensington Palace for at-risk homeless youth in 2013. As well as performing her own hits, she joined Prince William and singer Jon Bon Jovi on stage to belt out "Livin' on a Prayer". Just over ten years later, the Prince of Wales attended her sold-out concert at Wembley Stadium, proudly wearing a friendship bracelet made by his daughter.

♀ B2 · 🏠 Kensington Gardens, W8 4PX
🚇 Kensington Olympia · 🚇 Queensway, Notting Hill Gate
🕐 Hours vary, check website · Ⓦ hrp.org.uk

ALICE'S

Alice's ruby red façade never fails to lure shoppers to its doors. Located on the Portobello Road, a lively street in Notting Hill lined with charming antiques stores and pastel-hued homes, this 19th-century antiques store is the definition of beautifully organized chaos. Piles of wooden furniture and garish homeware decorate the entrance, leading to teetering towers of quirky bric-a-brac and crockery inside. Look familiar? Alice's featured in the family-friendly movie *Paddington 2*, albeit under the name of "Gruber's Antiques". The store also appeared in photos from Taylor's visit to London in 2012, where she was seen browsing antiques with friends. (It's rumoured the owners closed the store just for the singer.) If you're visiting on a Saturday, make the most of the Portobello Market just up the road, equally loved for its stalls laden with curiosities and retro clothes.

———

📍 B2 · 🏠 86 Portobello Road, W11 2QD · 🚇 Notting Hill Gate
🕐 10am–4pm Tue–Fri, 8am–3pm Sat · 📞 020 7229 8187

CASA CRUZ

It's easy to see why Casa Cruz is a favourite among royals and A-list celebrities. Tucked away in an affluent patch of Notting Hill, this discreet Argentinian restaurant is a top location for the rich and famous to catch up with friends. Reflective, foliage-framed windows deter eagle-eyed paparazzi from photographing intimate dinners, while parasols and overgrown plants shield guests on the terrace. Inside, Casa Cruz exudes luxury; soft lighting reveals velvet chairs, copper-clad walls and a floor-to-ceiling display of wine bottles. While the building itself appears modern, it's a Victorian-age structure that once served as a pub and managed to survive the Blitz. It also famously survived a public scolding for hosting singer Rita Ora's birthday bash in 2021, at the height of the COVID-19 pandemic. Taylor wasn't there then but she made her own visit to Casa Cruz in summer 2024 with a gaggle of high-profile pals in tow, including fashion designer Stella McCartney (*p26*) and actors Andrew Scott and Phoebe Waller-Bridge.

📍 B2 · 🏠 123a Clarendon Road, W11 4JG · 🚇 Latimer Road
🕐 6pm–midnight daily · Ⓦ casacruz.co.uk/london

EVENTIM APOLLO

Eventim Apollo, formerly known as Hammersmith Odeon and Hammersmith Apollo, is one of London's best-preserved entertainment venues. The impressive Art Deco building first opened its doors as a cinema, in 1932, and was later refitted as a spacious theatre and gig space. While it might not have the same seating capacity as more modern venues such as the O2 (*p80*), what it lacks in seats it makes up for in character thanks to its geometric tiles and elaborate ceiling. It's also hosted some of the biggest names in comedy, theatre and live music, from Brixton-born David Bowie to Aussie superstar Kylie Minogue. In 2010, Taylor added her name to this list by performing at BBC Radio 1's Switch Awards. Sparkling guitar in hand, she performed three of her latest hits at the time: "Love Story", "Speak Now" and "Mine". She was in good company too, with fellow American singer Katy Perry also performing. Want to see a live performance while you're in the city? Eventim Apollo is a solid option.

📍 A2 • 🏠 45 Queen Caroline Street, W6 9QH
🚇 Hammersmith • 🕐 Hours vary, check website • Ⓦ eventimapollo.com

WEMBLEY STADIUM

Wembley Stadium is Taylor's home from home. Or it certainly felt like it in 2024, when she became the first solo singer to perform at the London venue eight times in one tour. Not only that, but Taylor also performed here more than in any other city on the Eras Tour (yep, she really likes London). And it's not just her performance that impressed the crowds. The sheer size of Wembley is mind-blowing – it's the second-largest stadium in Europe with a whopping 90,000 seats and 2,618 toilets to boot. Special artwork was also commissioned to delight fans during Taylor's shows, with the Spanish Steps leading up the entrance being given a Taylor-themed makeover. Why not relive your favourite era with a behind-the-scenes stadium tour?

———————

📍 A1 • 🏠 Empire Way, Wembley, HA9 0WS
🚇 Wembley Stadium • 🚇 Wembley Park
🕐 Hours vary, check website • Ⓦ wembleystadium.com

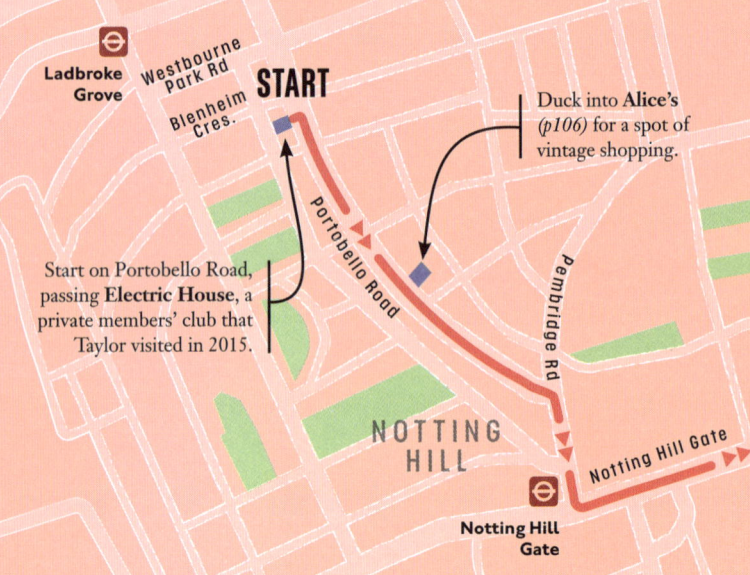

Ladbroke Grove

Westbourne Park Rd

Blenheim Cres.

START

Duck into **Alice's** *(p106)* for a spot of vintage shopping.

Portobello Road

Pembridge Rd

Start on Portobello Road, passing **Electric House**, a private members' club that Taylor visited in 2015.

NOTTING HILL

Notting Hill Gate

Notting Hill Gate

WALKING TOUR

WEST LONDON

Distance 5 km (3 miles) **Nearest Tube to Starting Point** Ladbroke Grove

If you want London à la Richard Curtis, take a walk through West London. It's here you'll find pastel-coloured townhouses, classy restaurants and a little place called Notting Hill, not to mention a few Taylor-related spots. It all wraps up at the Victoria and Albert Museum in South Kensington, once home to a Taylor-themed exhibition but pretty brilliant at any time of year.

250 metres
250 yards

North

BAYSWATER

Bayswater Road

Bayswater Road

KENSINGTON
GARDENS

HYDE
PARK

West Carriage Drive

Serpentine

The Broad Walk

Watch the birds soar above
the **Serpentine** - the
seagulls are very *1989
(Taylor's Version)*.

Round
Pond

Follow in Taylor's
footsteps and pay your
respects at the **Princess
Diana Memorial
Fountain**.

Rotton Row

Book a visit to
Kensington Palace
(p104), where Taylor
once played.

Kensington   Road

KNIGHTSBRIDGE

Exhibition Rd

Admire the **Royal Albert Hall**
from afar, one of London's most
elegant and historic venues.

END

Finish your walk at the **Victoria
and Albert Museum** *(p98)*, once
home to "The Songbook Trail".

South
Kensington

BEYOND LONDON

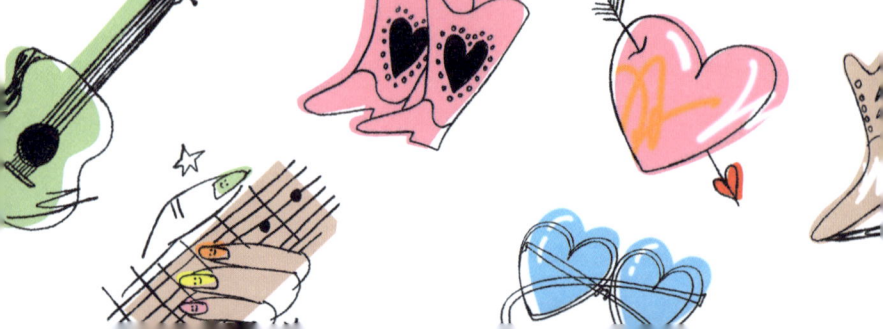

E | F

UK ON
THE MAP

100 km
100 miles

North ↑ | 1

SCOTLAND

Atlantic
Ocean

GLASGOW
p 130

EDINBURGH
p 132

North
Sea

NORTHERN
IRELAND

THE LAKE DISTRICT
p 126

Irish Sea

LIVERPOOL
p 124

IRELAND

HOLMES CHAPEL
p 122

ENGLAND

ALDEBURGH
p 134

2 | 2

WALES

THE COTSWOLDS
p 120

CARDIFF
p 136

LONDON
pp 12–113

English
Channel

ST IVES
p 138

E | | F

THE COTSWOLDS

Visiting the Cotswolds is one of the best ways to experience the English countryside. An Area of Outstanding Beauty, the region runs through five UK counties, including Oxfordshire and Gloucestershire. While they all have their own unique attractions, picturesque walks and local history, the pretty sandstone cottages and "wolds" (high open land or hills) unite them all. Taylor and American footballer Travis Kelce were rumoured to be staying in a mansion near Chipping Norton, Oxfordshire, in summer 2024 after a string of performances at Wembley Stadium (*p112*). Affectionately known as "Chippy" to the locals, the postcard-perfect town has fascinating antique stores, cute cafés and an old-fashioned sweet shop. After trying some traditional English sweets, why not see if you can get your hands on a packet of Taylor's beloved Squashies? Actor Judi Dench gifted Taylor packets of the pink-and-white striped "candy" on the set of *Cats* after hearing how much she liked them.

📍 F2 • 🚇 Cheltenham, Moreton in Marsh • Ⓦ cotswolds.com

HOLMES CHAPEL

A small Cheshire parish isn't somewhere you'd usually expect to find Taylor. Yet, in 2012, she was photographed in Holmes Chapel on a date with singer Harry Styles. The venue? A Chinese restaurant called Fortune City. The local spot was just a stone's throw from Harry's childhood home: Holmes Chapel. Today, the area has an influx of "Harries", with fans embarking on walking tours of his former stomping ground. Stops along the way include Mandeville's Bakery, where Harry worked as a teenager, and the impressive Twemlow Viaduct, a historic structure now affectionately known as "Harry's wall".

📍 F2 · 🚇 Holmes Chapel
Ⓦ hcpartnership.org.uk/harryshomevillagemap

LIVERPOOL

A UNESCO Creative City of Music, Liverpool is best known for giving the world The Beatles, though its musical legacy runs even deeper. From the Royal Liverpool Philharmonic (one of the UK's oldest orchestras) to hosting Eurovision 2023, this city knows how to put on a show. Talking of musical icons… Taylor chose Liverpool as the backdrop for her "I Can See You (Taylor's Version) (From the Vault)" music video. The video, starring actors Taylor Lautner and Joey King, spotlights several historic landmarks in Liverpool, including the Cunard Building and St George's Hall. Liverpool welcomed Taylor back in 2024 for the Eras Tour at Anfield Stadium, rolling out the red carpet, Taylor-style – not only were buildings decorated but the University of Liverpool held a "Tay Day" for fans, briefly earning the city the nickname "Taylor Town". The banners might be down now, but if you're a music fan, Liverpool is a must-visit.

📍 F2 · 🚇 Liverpool Lime Street · Ⓦ visitliverpool.com

THE LAKE DISTRICT

There are plenty of places in the UK where you can go for a walk, but none more spectacular than the Lake District. Home to glittering waters, England's highest mountain and picture-perfect villages, the region has inspired poets, painters and writers for generations – including, we like to think, Taylor. The star was first snapped visiting the Lake District with singer Harry Styles in 2012, when the duo made a flying visit to Bowness-on-Windermere, a small town overlooking Lake Windermere. Years later, Taylor returned during COVID-19, exchanging London for green peaks. Her trip here is thought to be the reason behind the song "The Lakes". So, if you're having a spot of writers' block, the Lake District might be the very best place to go.

───────────

📍 F2 · 🚇 Windermere · ⓦ visitlakedistrict.com

GLASGOW

Sure, London has the Thames *(p82)* but Glasgow has the River Clyde. This sweeping waterway cuts through the heart of Scotland's largest city, passing world-class museums, legendary music venues and a distillery or two. The stunning Victorian architecture only adds to the city's charm – though when Taylor visited in 2015, she went a tad more modern, lighting up Glasgow's OVO Hydro stadium on her *1989* tour with energetic choreography, synthy hits and a surprise family history lesson: she's got Scottish ancestry. While Taylor didn't add Glasgow as a stop for her 2024 tour, it didn't stop "Taylor fever" from coming to town. Glasgow Clyde College even held a 90-minute masterclass for fans to get up to speed before her Edinburgh shows *(p132)*. Meanwhile Glasgow-formed band The Blue Nile experienced an unexpected uplift in sales after being name-checked in her 2024 song "Guilty as Sin?". Proof, if ever needed, that in Glasgow, Taylor's impact is very much alive and kicking.

———

📍 E1 • 🚆 Glasgow Central • Ⓦ visitglasgow.com

EDINBURGH

Scotland's capital? Straight-up enchanting. Winding cobbled streets lead to wee coffee shops with friendly baristas and indie stores stocked with timeless tartan. The sights are impressive too. Beautiful landscaped parks sit below the stunning 11th-century Edinburgh castle, while further out of town Arthur's Seat, an ancient volcano, peers out across the North Sea. If you're here in summer, expect laughter, music and Fringe Festival chaos. This celebration of art and culture inevitably draws in spectacular crowds from across the world. And speaking of crowds... enter Taylor Swift. All three of her 2024 shows at Scottish Gas Murrayfield, Edinburgh's largest stadium, broke attendance records – and startled local scientists. Fans danced so hard to songs that the British Geological Survey recorded seismic activity up to 4 km (6 miles) away. Talk about being a force of nature.

———————

📍 F1 • 🚇 Edinburgh Waverley • ⓦ edinburgh.org

ALDEBURGH

Remember when Taylor dated Tom Hiddleston? Of course you do. The summer of "Hiddleswift" was a moment, with one of their most wholesome outings a golden hour beach stroll in Aldeburgh, Suffolk, with none other than Tom's seemingly delighted mother in tow. You might not have heard of Aldeburgh: most Londoners looking for a seaside escape head to Brighton or Margate, but they're missing a trick. The east coast of England is full of lovely seaside towns and rugged beaches, Aldeburgh being a prime example. There's musical heritage here, too: composer Benjamin Britten started the Aldeburgh music festival in 1948, and it's still held here every June – there's even a sculpture dedicated to Britten on the seafront. The controversial "Scallop" by artist Maggi Hambling looks kind of like a chrome *Swiftopecten swiftii* aka Swift's Scallop, which some fans believe inspired the opening of the Eras Tour. Coincidence? We think not.

♀ F2 · 🚇 Saxmundham, then bus · Ⓦ visitsuffolk.com

CARDIFF

Long gone are Cardiff's days of exporting coal; these days, the Welsh capital is all about importing good vibes – from enthusiastic uni students to dedicated sports and music fans. The city's got the perfect mix of old meets new, with the medieval Cardiff Castle sat right in the centre and several Victorian and Edwardian arcades offering some of the quirkiest shopping in the UK. Also in town is the Principality Stadium, home of Welsh rugby and the spot where Taylor made her Wales debut in 2024. She only played one night, but she left a lasting impression, greeting the crowd in Welsh (iconic) and making a sizeable donation to a Cardiff Foodbank charity, something she also did for various cities across the UK, including Liverpool *(p124)* and London *(p8)*. Short but sweet? Definitely. Unforgettable? You bet.

———

♀ F2 · 🚇 Cardiff Central · Ⓦ visitcardiff.com

ST IVES

The sand won't hurt your feelings in St Ives – but it might make you want to quit your day job for a life by the sea. With golden beaches, turquoise waters and decent waves, this Cornish coastal town is a dream. The town is also synonymous with art, after a colony of artists settled here in the 1920s. Today that legacy lives on at Tate St Ives, perched above pretty Porthmeor Beach with views as gorgeous as the art inside. Nearby, the fascinating Barbara Hepworth Museum and Sculpture Garden celebrates one of the 20th century's most important artists. Taylor and Joe Alwyn reportedly exchanged Nashville for St Ives in 2022, flying 6,440 km (4,000 miles) for a romantic three-day getaway. No sightings? No surprise. As someone who travelled to the stage in an adapted "cleaning cart" for her own 2023–2024 tour, Taylor's pretty creative when it comes to staying hidden.

📍 E2 • 🚇 St Ives • ⓦ visitcornwall.com

DIRECTORY

Want to make the most of your trip to London and the UK? Channel your inner mastermind and use the following resources to make your trip as memorable – and as fearless – as possible.

PERSONAL SECURITY

London is generally safe but petty crime (including mobile phone theft) does take place, especially in tourist areas. Use your common sense and be alert to your surroundings. If anything is stolen, report the crime as soon as possible to the nearest police station and ask for a copy of the crime report for insurance purposes.

www.btp.police.uk
The British Transport Police (BTP) covers crimes committed on the train, Tube, bus or tram. You can also text 61016 in a non-emergency.

www.met.police.uk
Report crimes online and view information about major police incidents in the city.

www.report-it.org.uk
A website for reporting hate crimes with a list of organizations that can help victims.

SAFE SPACES

London is a diverse and inclusive city, but should you feel uneasy at any point and want to find your community, there are spaces catering to different genders, ethnicities and religions.

www.blackownedlondon.com
A curated online guide to London's Black-owned businesses.

www.jw3.org.uk
An all-encompassing cultural centre for London's Jewish communities.

londonmandir.baps.org
A Hindu temple and a welcoming cultural centre for all.

www.muslimsinbritain.org
The definitive guide to mosques and Muslim community spaces in the UK.

www.stonewall.org.uk
Charity offering support for the LGBTQ+ community, as well as a list of services.

HEALTH

The UK has a world-class healthcare system that provides free emergency care for all, regardless of their nationality. Non-emergency care does come at a cost, however, so make sure you take out comprehensive health insurance before you visit. EU citizens can receive medical treatment free of charge if they have a valid European Health Insurance Card (EHIC).

www.boots-uk.com
The UK's leading pharmacy-led retailer, with over 1,800 stores across the country.

www.guysandstthomas.nhs.uk
An A&E department and walk-in urgent care centre on the south bank.

www.nhs.uk
The website for the UK's National Health Service (NHS), full of advice and a list of health centres.

TRAVEL ADVICE

Getting around the city and the UK is relatively easy. Before you travel – and while you're here – make sure to check for disruption, as well as the latest UK regulations.

www.gov.uk/guidance/apply-for-an-electronic-travel-authorisation-eta
Check if you need to secure an Electronic Travel Authorisation (ETA) before flying to the UK.

www.nationalrail.co.uk
Purchase train tickets, check timetables and plan your cross-country trips.

www.tfl.gov.uk
Plan city-wide journeys and check for delays on the Transport for London (TfL) website.

www.thetrainline.com
Book tickets for local train journeys and bigger day trips.

ACCESSIBILITY

Though plenty of change is needed, cities across the UK are always improving when it comes to accessibility. The following resources will assist in helping your journey run smoothly.

accessmap.nationalrail.co.uk
An interactive resource for checking train station accessibility before you travel.

www.euansguide.com
A forum for disabled access reviews on restaurants, theatres and other attractions, by and for people with specific requirements.

www.scope.org.uk
Charity providing advice and support on how to get help on public transport.

www.tfl.gov.uk/transport-accessibility
Transport for London's official website and accessible journey planner.

www.tourismforall.co.uk
A central source of information with useful travel and accommodation tips.

INDEX

Project Editor Sarah Allen
Senior Editor Lucy Richards
Designers Gemma Doyle, Kei Ishimaru
Proofreader Stephanie Evans
Indexer Cathy Heath
Jacket Designer Gemma Doyle
Illustrator Jordan Andrew Carter
**Rights and Permissions
Specialist** Priya Singh
Senior Cartographic Editor
James Macdonald
Publishing Assistant Simona Velikova
Production Editor David Almond
**Senior Production
Controller** Samantha Cross
Managing Art Editor Gemma Doyle
Editorial Director Hollie Teague
Art Director Max Pedliham
Publishing Director Georgina Dee

First published in Great Britain in 2025 by
Dorling Kindersley Limited 20 Vauxhall
Bridge Road, London SW1V 2SA

The authorised representative in the EEA is
Dorling Kindersley Verlag GmbH. Arnulfstr.
124, 80636 Munich, Germany

Copyright © 2025 Dorling Kindersley Limited
A Penguin Random House Company
25 26 27 28 10 9 8 7 6 5 4 3 2 1
001–354560–Sep/2025

A CIP catalogue record for this book
is available from the British Library.
A catalog record for this book is
available from the Library of Congress.

ISBN: 978-0-2417-7439-7

Printed and bound in China.
www.dk.com

Author
Sarah Allen is an editor and writer at the
award-winning DK Travel. Based in South
London, she's been listening to Taylor's music
since her early teens and loves nothing more
than decoding Taylor's lyrics on walks around
the city and road trips.

Pic Credits
The publisher would like to thank the
following for their kind permission to
reproduce their photographs:

Alamy Stock Photo: Simon Turner 31; Alex Segre
32; Alex Segre 57; Cath Harries 58; Lee Martin
61; Benjamin John 110; Vuk Valcic 113;
Mark Waugh 123.

Benihana Chelsea: 96.

Bob Bob Ricard: 17.

Casa Cruz: 107.

Depositphotos Inc: brians101 138.

Dreamstime.com: AlenaKravchenko 70;
A Faustov 76; Ac Manley 87; Whitcomberd 127;
Jingmin310 137.

Getty Images: Jeff Greenberg 90.

Getty Images / iStock: David Taljat 14; OGULCAN
AKSOY 24–25; Patrickistock 27; Paul Hayward 28;
cmspic 35; David Ramirez 41; Anthony Bressy 45;
Jan-Otto 46–47; Adrien Delforge 48;
coldsnowstorm 62–63; Moonstone Images 66;
phaustov73; Abdul Shakoor 80; John Mouchet 84;
fotoVoyager 88–89; brightstars 100; Jelena
Mbugua 102–103; SangHyunPaek 105; Alla
Tsyganova106; SolStock 128–129; Drimafilm 130.

HAWKSMOOR SEVEN DIALS: 21.

MCC: Jed Leicester 38.

Unsplash: Sabrina Mazzeo 2; Nik Guiney 6; James
Kirkup 13; Hulki Okan Tabak 18; Adrien Delforge
22; Sander Crombach 83; Andrea Desantis 99;
Julia Solonina 118; George Ciobra 120; Phil Kiel
124; Connor Mollison 133; David Tip 134.

ZSL London Zoo: 42.

All other images © **Rob Greig.**